Christmas

Twelve Poems to Tell and Share

ex libris

Candlestick Press

Published by:

Candlestick Press,
Diversity House, 72 Nottingham Road, Arnold, Nottingham NG5 6LF
www.candlestickpress.co.uk

Design and typesetting by Craig Twigg

Printed by Ratcliff & Roper Print Group, Nottinghamshire, UK

Cover illustration © Sarah Young, 2022
www.sarahyoung.co.uk

Candlestick Press monogram © Barbara Shaw, 2008

© Candlestick Press, 2022

Donation to Starlight Children's Foundation
www.starlight.org.uk

ISBN 978 1 913627 15 7

Acknowledgements

Thanks are due to the authors listed below for kind permission to use their poem,
all of which are as yet unpublished:

Abeer Ameer, Panya Banjoko, Kathryn Bevis, Jim Carruth, Linda France, John
Freeman, Arjunan Manuelpillai, Helen Mort, Victoria Punch, Kostya Tsolakis,
Rory Waterman and Tamar Yoseloff.

Contents

A Tale for Christmas Eve Night

The long night's moon throws silver sheets over
the chimney pots, the buttercross, the coppice
and the stream. A new frost splinters, spreads her
fingers, etches each branch so bright against

the dark. Tidy as made beds, the meadows
dream of wheat. Trees stretch their roots a little
deeper. In the choir, children stamp, milky
and restless as calves in the barn. They sing

for Christmas to come. Listen. The night throbs
with a new stillness. Love is being born,
crying out for joy. See its star rise up the lane,
and through the copse, across the drowsy fields.

Kathryn Bevis

Telling It Slant

The story
      re-gifted to me, wrapped
           in tired gold   concerns
               my dead step-grandad, Alf
                   (prolific whistler
                   60-a-day smoker
                   yellow-fingered
                   bald)
how he came back from The Arkwright
      with my dad   settled
           to carve the turkey

but the gin had   loosened
      his wrists so with every   stroke
           of the too-blunt knife he
                 leaned a little further
                     to the right

until he was diagonal
      – a knife himself –
           then spark out on the floor
                snoring   like hell

and I don't remember
      but it sounds true
           and   all my life
                I've been trying to write

about Alf and his bumbling kindness
and my childish disdain
    but all my thoughts slip sideways

and memory is sharp   nearly painful,
        a lightning bolt
            a dropped
            knife

Helen Mort

The Gift

It's 1958 and there he is – Faruq of Baghdad.
Ten-year-old stamp collector with quiffed hair,
dishdasha top button done up. He's a sight to behold.
He's going somewhere. Ordered. Precise. Leader of the pack.

But today he's distraught – his stamp collection's lost.
He's searched everywhere. His younger brother, showing no care,
with his greasy hands and stamp-creasing fingers, took the album
to school, left it there. The stamps are gone. Faruq is ruined.

Ameer feels the pain of his hero, two years his senior.
Unschooled in the art of stamp collecting, but full of enthusiasm,
he imagines giving Faruq the perfect gift to lift his spirits.
He finds what he's looking for in his father's desk drawer

and, grabbing scissors with zeal, he cuts the pages of visa stamps
from his father's passport. He's careful to keep the serrated edges intact.
Ameer runs to find Faruq, proudly hands over the cut-outs.
But there's no glint in Faruq's eyes. Even the shine in his hair has gone.

Visa stamps are standard issue, far too plain for philately, Ameer's told.
Some years later, Ameer is a student in England. He spends his shillings
and pence on airmail envelopes and thin paper. He needs many stamps
to send letters home. He's lonely here – an outsider in Carlisle.

He tries to write light of the darkness without an end.
Each letter begins in the name of God. *Bismillah*. Once a month,
he saves enough to make an international call. Too few glorious minutes
of *Salaam, Shlonkum? Mishtaqeen Wallah*
　　　　　　　before the bump back to earth on the click of the receiver.

It's 1966; Ameer's at the post office again. There's a new set of stamps.
It's all the rage – the first issue of a Christmas edition. He's intrigued
by this jolly season so strange. A snowman. A king. Children's drawings
now world famous. He buys two sets; one for his parents,

another for Faruq of Baghdad. The darkness clears as the teens
exchange letters, year after year. Soon, they have families of their own.
Decades and their parents pass. A few pirates and emperors
are overthrown and at last in 2004, Ameer can return to Iraq.

In his father's drawer, he finds the letters he wrote. Christmas stamps
since 1966, his own children's drawings. The passport with cut pages –
leftovers from the offering to his hero. He smiles at a self eager to please.
He still buys the Christmas sets each year. Keeps his passport
                                        under lock and key.

Abeer Ameer

Arboreal

My father – a mischievous man with delusions
of grandeur and Neapolitan charisma,
given to stories – told me his grandparents' names
were Mary and Joseph. Only nine at the time,
I pencilled them in on our scant family tree
before catching the twinkle in his merry eye.
After that, every Christmas, not knowing
where I belonged, I'd gaze at the nativity,
away in the manger – pastoral, beatific –
wanting the holy family's story to be mine.

My mother, down to earth, no nonsense, preferred
to blend into the background, almost invisible –
but at Christmas what made her happy was a tree.
Every year we'd trek deep in the wilderness
beyond the railway line, her swinging the big saw
as if it were a handbag. Under cover of dusk,
Mam at one end and me at the other, we'd carry
the chosen one home. Our trees were pine, not bought
spruce – long-needled, rangy, poached – hung
with mottled post-war baubles, paper lanterns.

Short of any other narrative to make sense
of the world we find ourselves in and to venerate
our lost ancestors – émigrés, survivors –
I tell my sons these stories in the dark of winter:
our origin myths, borrowed and stolen, a forest
of rootless, ungovernable evergreen trees.

Linda France

The WPIX Yule Log

never died, never needed kindling, blazing
inside the TV, it flickered into apartments,
fire escapes decked with tinsel, fake firs,
while we crooned like Bing about the white stuff.

Maybe it still burned after we switched off
and went to bed – eternal like the candle
Our Lady cradled at her eponymous church,
manger strewn with trash from passing cars.

And every year the flame returned, miraculous,
in the glow of analog screens, accompanied
by *Joy to the World* and *Hark the Herald Angels* –

inviting us to gather around the console
with loved ones, cups of eggnog spiked with rum,
to catch pretend snow on our tongues, and sing.

Tamar Yoseloff

The light-up snowman on the balcony

Cheap plastic thing. Through smear-free
glass, your gentle glow allows the boy

to survey his room – this ordered universe –
as he falls asleep. The cared-for spines

of illustrated books: Greek myths, great
civilisations, the illustrious lives of explorers

and conquerors. The silver-plated protector-
saints above the headboard. On the white-top desk,

stapler, hole-punch, magnifying glass,
laid out neatly side by side. Every colour

in the pencil holder, sharpened to a point. Spikes
that wall a fortress. The slatted wardrobe

doors, behind which everything – t-shirts, pyjamas,
underwear, socks – is ironed to perfection.

You clutch a candy cane – striped red and white
like a barber's pole or barrier tape – look smart,

the boy thinks, in your black top hat, green
scarf wrapped snuggly round your neck.

Your affable smile reminds him
of that flying snowman in the film. The boy

has his pilot dad for that. Dad who sees
to the tree: from picking it with the care

of an emperor choosing his heir, to hand-
sawing it apart, on the Feast of the Lights,

to be fed, branch by frayed branch,
to the fireplace. And the smell of burnt spruce

lingers for days. Mum will pack away the decorations,
carefully wrap the gilded baubles she's had

since childhood. She expects the boy to pass them
down to his own kids – those vague-shaped

creatures, still viable in his mind. Each year he asks
for you, Snowman, to be kept out: *All year, yes.*

It's a queer request. *Imagine*, Mum laughs,
the light-up snowman on the balcony

– in July! What will the neighbours think?
Such unorthodox desire.

Kostya Tsolakis

My Father's Soil
(24th December 2013)

Christmas Eve, and at our doorstep
a basket of Golden Wonders newly dug
by my brother who lifted them alone
bending tear-blind into a bitter wind
as it strengthened all day to a storm.

These are taken from my father's soil –
he, who nurtured each from seed,
put in hard hours through the seasons
till they were fully grown and ready to eat.
For years we have received his harvest

left hanging on the door, bags heaving
with cabbages, carrots, wrist-thick leeks
the flowering of a vegetable bouquet.
There can be no better feast in life
than the gifts that only loved ones bring.

Tomorrow, he won't be at our table
surrounded by the fruits of all his labours
to lay out his beloved mash and roast
watching our sad longing devour it all:
his love for us, his loss, his final crop.

Jim Carruth

A Homecoming

For once the neighbours are not quarrelling.
Leaving the fridge to fill the quiet
with its groaning protest at being overloaded.

The children have found their own
parts of the world to learn what love is.

Gone are the days
when they were tangled around my feet.
And I wished instead to be swathed in silence.

To count things I should have done
(or not), to remove my warrior mask, to retreat.

The dent in the settee tells me
I've been brooding far too long.

Soon the crunching of boots
on the gravelled path
will come.

For now, breath held,
I wait for doorbell's jingle
and for the greatest gift of all,
feeding their hungry ears.

Panya Banjoko

In Walked Father Christmas

How much do I need to tell you so you know
what it meant when I saw the door handle turn
from inside the sitting room where I waited
with Mummy and Daddy and when slowly
the door opened and in walked Father Christmas?
There was no mistaking him, his long red cloak
trimmed with fur like new soft-fallen snow,
his hood pulled down so that between that
and his equally snowy beard and whiskers
I could hardly see his face, but after all
I didn't need to, he was who he was.
In a fuzzy old man's voice he answered
my eager treble greeting, and put down
his hessian sack, like the ones potatoes
were sometimes lugged home from the market in,
and began to take a parcel from it.
Presents! With deliberate, thoughtful movements
Father Christmas loomed in my direction
mumbling that this one was for me, but something
was badly wrong, I couldn't let this happen.
We weren't all here. We must wait for Michael,
I said, we can't begin without him.
When you're four, eight years is a big gap
between siblings. My brother was my hero.
Father Christmas looked uncertain what to do.
It was stalemate. Somehow he and my parents
must have very slowly persuaded me
that we could save Michael's presents for him
and let Santa get on with giving us ours.
It was a pleasure to watch him pass them
with muffled words to each of us, and leave
a heap of gifts for Michael, but a mixed one,
a fraction of the joy it should have been.
His sack empty at last, Santa plodded out.

Five minutes later the door handle turned
again, and this time Michael came in. You missed
Father Christmas! I told him. He was here!

John Freeman

The Homemaker's Tale

God rest ye, merry gentleman.
  Let nothing you dismay:
your wife is making dinner just
  like every other day –
watch *Gremlins* then *The Snowman* then
  The Best Man Holiday.
    O tidings of comfort and joy,
    Comfort and joy.
    O tidings of comfort and joy.

Your son won't leave his bedroom and
  your daughter's in a state:
her boyfriend went out late last night and
  got off with her mate.
She ponders how to kill him as
  the photos circulate.
    O tidings of comfort and joy,
    Comfort and joy.
    O tidings of comfort and joy.

But all of them get hungry and
  it's three o'clock, then four,
and you've snacked on wine and wafers then
  some more wine then some more,
but finally it's ready. You pull
  down the oven door.
    O tidings of comfort and joy,
    Comfort and joy.
    O tidings of comfort and joy.

The sprouts are soggy batteries.
  The turkey tastes alright
but soon you'll drop the mince pies, see
  the pudding catch alight,

and swear, evoke the Holy Child,
   then serve Angel Delight.
      O tidings of comfort and joy,
      Comfort and joy.
      O tidings of comfort and joy.

Rory Waterman

25th December, 6.15am

It's the morning I love most,
the sun, nervous to see us,
meandering through
a monkey climber's branches.
My father and I already up,
disappearing into sarongs.
His is a turquoise silk,
mine, bottle green cotton.
We barely speak between
the coffee sips from two
1999 secret Santa gifts.
I'm in the literature supplement,
he is in the business one.
I talk of poems, he describes
the rise in property prices.
It makes me wonder
if Joseph and Jesus
sat together like this.
Whether Jesus feigned
interest in his father's
next bespoke rocking chair.
Whether he was always out,
late for supper, hardly home.
Whether his father, Joseph,
tired of listening to him go on
about his latest miracle.
I want to tell my father
how much I love him but
settle for showing him how to
listen to podcasts on his phone.
Later, the whole family
jam into the car for church.
For the whole sermon
there's no mention of Joseph.

But you can see him,
in the nativity, behind Mary,
quietly planning where
they would sleep tomorrow.

Arjunan Manuelpillai

While the three wise men dreamed

And travelled, camels packed, living by starlight, an open invite
to the king's table – the women (wise, unnamed) were
also there. Birthing and bathing and breasting their babes.
She, now wife, now mothering. And the women tell
how to be strong – when to push, how to survive.
What to do with bloody rags, how to wash when
you're awash with the milk coming in. With sleep
deprivation. The wise men have gold. The women have
straw, bedding, practical wisdom; how breastmilk soothes dry
skin, when baby needs burping, how to rest, how to
cope best – and once baby is here, once the squeal
has been heard, he is glad tidings, great joy. But
what I want is to sit down, look her straight
in the eye, and say: Well done, Mary. Well Done.

Victoria Punch